The Chinese Art of Face Reading

The Chinese Art of Face Reading

Evelyn Lip

TIMES BOOKS INTERNATIONAL
Singapore • Kuala Lumpur

Photographs courtesy of the Straits Times Press
(1975) Pte Ltd

© **Illustrations Evelyn Lip**

© **1989 Times Editions Pte Ltd**

Published by Times Books International
an imprint of Times Editions Pte Ltd
Times Centre
1 New Industrial Road
Singapore 1953

Times Subang
Lot 46, Subang Hi-Tech Industrial Park
Batu Tiga
40000 Shah Alam
Selangor Darul Ehsan
Malaysia

Reprinted 1991, 1992, 1995

Set in Baskerville 10 over 12 points

Printed in Singapore

ISBN 981 204 119 2

For Francis, Kenny and Jacqueline

Contents

The face of Zhong Kui, a scholar of the Tang dynasty, was so grotesque
that the emperor disqualified him although he topped the imperial examinations.

Preface

My article on *ming xiang* 命相 or face reading was published in 1985 (in the book *Chinese Beliefs and Superstitions*). The interesting response from my readers has prompted me to write further and elaborate on this Chinese art of physiognomy which goes as far back as 2000 years ago.

For centuries the Chinese painted the facial features of opera characters with brilliant colours and shades to portray the characters more vividly. They did so because they believed that facial features portrayed the character of a person. There were all kinds of faces: evil, kind, sad, happy, weak, powerful, scholastic, martial, stupid, intelligent and so on.

In Chinese history, there were occasions when the face of a person affected his or her fortune. Zhong Kui, a scholar of the Tang dynasty, committed suicide because although he topped the imperial examination, the emperor disqualified him because of his grotesque facial features. Wang Zhao Jun, a great beauty, was not selected to be a concubine because the court artist disfavoured her and painted her badly.

For the Chinese, the face not only reveals certain personality traits and the spirit of a person, but also his past, present and future. And through the thousands of years of their civilisation, they have evolved the art of reading the face for a person's character and fortune.

Ming xiang or face reading is so important that it is yearly illustrated and repeated in the *Tong Shu*, the Chinese Almanac.

This book is an introduction to the art of face reading. It explains the significance of facial features and how they influence the wellbeing and fortune and reveal the personality traits of a person. There are also detailed studies of facial features of some famous faces from 551 B.C. to the present day, comparing their milestones with their facial features. The book also contains over 200 drawings which help readers identify the facial features discussed.

The book is written for all those who are interested in Chinese culture and beliefs, in fate and divination, and in face reading.

Acknowledgements

I wish to thank my friends, readers and publishers who have given me encouragement and help to make this a readable and enjoyable book. I am grateful for the help given to me in my search for photographic images of famous people. Special thanks go to Isabel Yeo, librarian, and Alice Tan, researcher, of the Straits Times Library.

I wish to thank the Straits Times Press for giving permission to my publisher to publish the photographs in this book. My own illustrations (more than 200) are based on the theory of *ming xiang*. However, many sketches of the famous are based on photographs taken by others. I owe my gratitude to those who have taken these photographs.

Last but not least I wish to thank all those who in one way or another inspired me to complete this book.

額廣耳珠　頭圓足厚　眉清目秀　地閣豐肥　鼻垂懸膽　面方背厚　宛如龜

Translation:

Forehead wide, ear lobe round and fleshy, head round, eyebrows well-delineated, eyes clear and refined, chin full, nose tip round like a gall bladder, face square and back fleshy like a tortoise.

1 Introduction

The theory of *ming xiang* 命相 or face reading is deeply rooted in Chinese culture. To the Chinese mind, fate is predestined but *yun* 运 (lucky and unlucky spells) can be changed if man knows in advance the approach of ill luck and searches for ways to avert its ill effects on time. On the other hand it may be easier for him to accept his fate and *yun* or to act positively so that the ill effects may be reduced if he understands the forces that mould him. Moreover, the Chinese have the philosophy of taking things calmly instead of rashly, going with nature instead of against it, knowing one's fault instead of ignoring it. Thus the proverb *zhi zi zhi ming* 知自之明, it is advantageous to know one's own virtues and vices, fate and fortune.

Although man is defenceless against destiny he is still better off knowing the odds, rather than being completely ignorant. Not only does he find out about himself, but also of those around him. To him knowing the facial features of one's family members, business associates, friends and even foes is getting an insight of their personality traits and intellectual capacity. This makes it easier to relate to them. After all, understanding of human nature is a fundamental of social relationship.

The art of face reading was evolved by the Chinese since 2,000 years ago. It was and still is used for analysing a man's intellectual capacity, personality traits and fortune. It is also related to the basic Chinese philosophical theory of the workings of the Five Elements.* The facial features are related to the internal organs of the body and

---

* The Five Elements are the five forces of nature, conceived by the Chinese as early as the 4th century B.C., and are designed in the sequence gold, wood, water, fire and earth.

15

can be classified under the Five Elements (gold, wood, water, fire and earth) as shown in the list below.

Facial features	Elements	Internal organs
forehead	fire	kidneys
nose	gold	lungs
mouth/lips	earth	spleen
ears	water	kidneys
eyes	wood	liver
eyebrows	fire	kidneys

Note: if the facial features are deformed the related internal organs may be defective.

In Chinese face reading it is not just the examination of facial features to determine whether or not the features are beautiful or wholesome. It is also necessary to gauge whether or not the facial features are 'compatible' in terms of their Element. As we know, water is compatible with wood, wood with fire, fire with earth, earth with gold and gold with water. But earth opposes water, water opposes fire, fire opposes gold, gold opposes wood and wood opposes earth. Take for example the ears which are of water Element. If the ears are long, fleshy and well-shaped, though the eyes may not be perfectly well-formed, the fortune of the person depicted by the eyes (from 37 to 38 years of age) may still be good. This is because the eyes are of wood Element and compatible with the ears (water Element). On the other hand if the ears are well-formed but the facial feature of opposing Element, the eyebrows, are not, the ears cannot influence the fortune of the person depicted by the eyebrows, that is, from 33 to 34 years of age.

However, the art of face reading was not based on theories alone, but also on years of observations by the face reading masters of old.

Chinese face readers also believe that the personality of a person is noticeably shown on the face. If a man is confident his eyes are bright and he looks you in the eye. If he is nervous he stammers and perhaps looks sideways. Courage, frankness, industry, or cowardice, deception and laziness too can be detected by close examination of the face and head. The compassion of a man is revealed by his countenance.

Physical behaviour reflects mental state. Emotional reactions are expressed through the face and body. Therefore past experiences, emotions and expressions mould facial features. Traumatic and sad experiences in life leave permanent marks on the face just as physical injuries leave behind scars.

As a person grows from childhood to old age, not only are there physical changes in body build, but also in facial features as well. The biological maturation goes hand in hand with the psychological and physical development including facial maturation. Problems, challenges, anxieties, dissatisfactions, boredom, excitement, enjoyment, hardships, joys and happiness are registered on the face and these experiences also change facial features. Therefore a face reader can actually read a face and tell the past. A good face reader even forecasts the future based on the features of the face and the shape of the face.

The Chinese face reader assesses a person's character and fortune in terms of facial features and how balanced the features are in relation to the shape of the face. For example if the head is pointed and the face is thin and small, the personality traits may be insociability and timidity and the person may even encounter ill luck. If the cheek bones are high but the nose is flat the personality traits may be ill discipline and boastfulness. If the eyes are small in comparison to the overall face the personality traits may be distrustfulness and dishonesty. If the mouth is small in comparison to the face, the person may be harsh and mean. He may even live a short life. If the cheek bones are too broad the personality trait may be heartlessness.

Determining personality and predicting behaviour through face reading is most effective by examining the eyes, ears, mouth and nose of a person because they are the sensory receptors. Vision is the most important sense because it informs the brain about the physical environment resulting in some form of behaviour on the part of the recipient. Eye contact is a very important facial gesture through which behavioural and emotional state can be assessed. (See sketch of a murderer and the photo of an intelligent, happy person).

Below is a summary of the fortune of a person at different ages as revealed by different facial features. The age refers to the age of a person according to the Chinese lunar calendar. The Chinese believe that the moment a child is born, he or she is already one year old. Also, a person is a year older not on one's birthday, but on the first

This man murdered a lorry driver in 1985. Note the irregular shape of his eyes, eyebrows, cheeks and ears. (Sketch drawn from photograph from the Straits Times *files.)*▼

Hong Kong actress Kwan Shan Mei has a well-shaped face, brilliant eyes, strong cheek bones and full-formed features.

day of the lunar new year. For example, if a person is born on the eve of the lunar new year, he is one year old, and the following day, he is two years old. Generally, to get one's age according to the Chinese lunar calendar, a year is added to the age of the person in that year (ie, according the the Western calendar). Refer to first diagram on page 20 to identify parts of the face.

Huo xing 火星 (top part of forehead) depicting the destiny of age 15 should be regular in form, smooth in profile and without marks or cuts.

Tian zhong 天中 (upper forehead below *huo xing*) depicting the luck of age 16 should be full and smooth although its bone structure can be slightly concave, and *tian ting* 天庭 (mid forehead below *tian zhong*) should also be smooth and free from moles. Similarly, *fu jiao* 辅角 (right and left upper temples) and *bian cheng* 边城 (right and left upper outer temples) should also be smooth and free from marks and moles. The bone structure of the entire forehead should be slightly concave (see chapter on foreheads).

Zhong zheng 中正 (lower forehead) is quite a prominent part of the forehead. It denotes the luck of age 25 and the profession and career destiny. It should be free from deformity and blemishes.

Yin tang 印堂 (area between the eyebrows) depicts the luck during the age of 28. It is sometimes called *ming tang* 命堂 because it refers to a critical point in life. Any defective marks or deformity indicate difficulties and ill health that threaten life.

The luck for the age of 30 is revealed on the *shan lin* 山林 (right and left lower temples). Defects occurring on this area depicts failure and poor luck. Above the eyebrows and just below the *shan lin* are the *ling yun* 凌云 which together with the *fan xia* 繁霞 (eyebrows) depict the wellbeing of 31 to 34, the quality and length of life. Eyebrows for females should be long, arched and refined and for males, should be long, hairy and well-formed (see chapter on eyebrows).

The destiny of ages 35 to 40 is depicted by the eyes. If the eyelids are thick, inheritance may be quite substantial. Generally eyes should be well-shaped and clear (see chapter on eyes). *Tai yin* 太阴 and *tai yang* 太阳 are the inner corner of the right eye and inner corner of the left eye respectively. They should be well-set and clear of moles and defects. Bulging or deformed, they indicate short life span. *Zhong yin* 中阴 and *zhong yang* 中阳 are the right and left eyes (see chapter on the eyes). They should be free from green or red veins.

The destiny of ages 41 to 50 is revealed by the shape and structure of the nose. The area of nose between the eyes is called *shan gen* 山根 and depicts the luck of age 41. Freckles on this area depict impatience. The left and right *jing she* 精舍 (areas of face above wings of the nose) depict the luck of 42. If they are greenish or greyish calamity may befall upon the person. *Nien shang* 年上 (area of nose below *shan gen*) and *shou shang* 寿上 (area of nose below *nien shang*) are important areas as they are in the middle portion of the nose which represents luck and ability. They should be sizeable and well-shaped (see chapter on nose). A straight and strong *nien shang* portrays ability and good fortune whereas a crooked or soft one portrays ill luck and complacency.

The left and right *quan* 颧 (left and right cheeks) depict the luck of 46 and 47. *Quan* should be full, prominent and free of defective marks. Its bone should not be too pronounced.

Zhun tou 準头 (the tip of the nose) is an important part of the nose depicting the destiny of 48. It should be round, well-developed and fleshy. Thin and weak *zhun tou* depicts poverty and disappointments. Hooked *zhun tou* depicts a vicious nature. *Lan tai* 兰台 (the right and left wings of the nose) should be well shaped so that the nostrils are not exposed (see chapter on nose).

The areas surrounding the mouth portray the luck from the age of 51 to 57 (see chapter on mouth). *Ren zhong* 仁中 (depression above

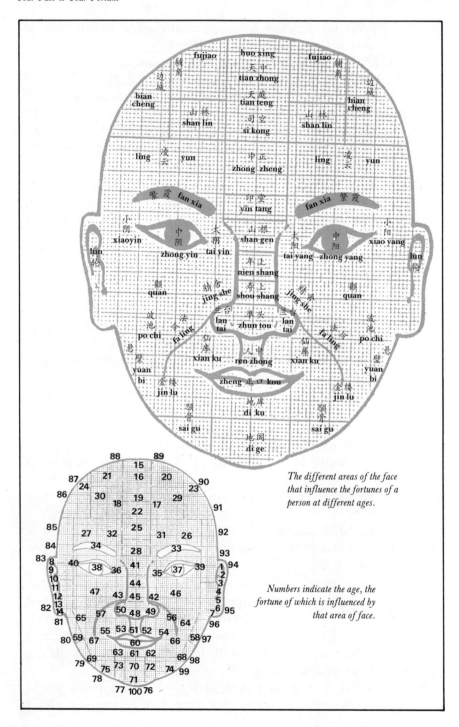

The different areas of the face that influence the fortunes of a person at different ages.

Numbers indicate the age, the fortune of which is influenced by that area of face.

upper lip) should be deep, balanced and well-shaped to depict longevity and good fortune at the age of 51. The luck from age 52 to 55 is spelt out on the areas to the left and right of the *ren zhong*. These areas, the *xian ku* 仙库 , should be well-formed without protrusions or depressions. The left and right *fa ling* 法令 (lines on the inner cheeks) depict the luck of ages 56 and 57 and the length of life span. They should be fairly deep and pronounced at the ages of 56 and 57.

The mouth governs the luck at age 60 (see chapter on mouth). The colour of the lips should be red and the thickness should be balanced otherwise the person may not live a very long life. Balanced lips with good colour indicate brilliance and fame. Teeth should be even and not protruding, concave or convex. Even the number of teeth signifies luck or ill fortune. For the male it is good to have 31 teeth (a *yang* number) but for the female it is not so (30, a *yin* number, is better).

The cheeks and chin reveal the destiny of a person from the age of 58 to 81 (with the exception of age 60). The areas known as the *xuan bi* 悬壁 (the part of cheek below the ear) govern the destiny of 58 and 59. These areas should be full and the colour even (without freckles) to indicate good health and luck. The wellbeing of ages 61 to 63 is depicted on the *di ku* 地库 (area below mouth). It should be full and fair in colour. The luck of 64 and 65 is spelt out by the areas immediately outside the left and right *fa ling*. If there are lines crossing these areas then there may be problems that take one by surprise.

The left and right *jin lu* 金娄 (the lower tips of *fa ling*) govern the ages 66 and 67. They should be full and not crossed by lines. The left and right jaws depict the luck at 68 and 69 respectively. These areas should not have green or grey patches on them.

The destiny of ages 70 to 73 is revealed on the chin. This area should be well-formed and free from defects (see chapter on cheeks and chin). From the age of 74 to 75 a person's luck is assessed by looking at the left and right *sai gu* 颐骨 (jaw bones) which should be neither too narrow nor too broad. If they are so large or broad that they can be seen from the back of the face, they indicate stubbornness and possible cruelty.

The areas of influence that govern the destiny from ages 76 to 100 are shown on the second diagram on facing page and in chart A.

The at-a-glance chart on pages 22 to 24 shows the areas of face to look at for luck and destiny from 1 to 75 years of age. This chart is read together wih the diagrams on page 20.

Chart A: Areas influencing fortune from 76 to 100 years old

Age	Area
76 to 81	jaws
82 to 83	ears
84 to 85	eyebrows
86 to 91	forehead
92 to 93	eyebrows
94 to 95	ears
96 to 99	jaws
100	left ear

Chart B: Areas influencing fortune from 1 to 75 years old

Age	Area of face
1 to 7	left *lun* 轮 (left ear) for males right *lun* (right ear) for females
7 to 14	right *lun* (right ear) for males left *lun* (left ear) for females
15	*huo xing* 火星 (top of forehead)
16 to 19	*tian zhong* 天中 (upper forehead) to *tian ting* 天庭 (mid forehead)
20	left *fu jiao* 辅角 (left upper temple)
21	right *fu jiao* (right upper temple)
22	*si kong* 司空 (lower middle forehead)
23	left *bian cheng* 边城 (left upper outer temple)
24	right *bian cheng* (right upper outer temple)

Age	Area of face
25	*zhong zheng* (lower forehead)
26 & 31	left *ling yun* 凌云 (area above left eyebrow)
27 & 32	right *ling yun* (area above right eyebrow)
28	*yin tang* 印堂 (area between eyebrows)
29	left *shan lin* 山林 (left lower temple)
30	right *shan lin* (right lower temple)
33	left *fan xia* 繁霞 (left eyebrow)
34	right *fan xia* (right eyebrow)
35	*tai yang* 太阳 (inner corner of left eye)
36	*tai yin* 太阴 (inner corner of right eye)
37	*zhong yang* 中阳 (left eye)
38	*zhong yin* 中阴 (right eye)
39	*xiao yang* 小阳 (outer corner of left eye)
40	*xiao yin* 小阴 (outer corner of right eye)
41	*shan gen* 山根 (area of nose between the eyes)
42	left *jing she* 精舍 (area above left wing of nose)
43	right *jing she* (area above right wing of nose)
44	*nien shang* 年上 (area of nose below *shan gen*)
45	*shou shang* 寿上 (area of nose below *nien shang*)
46	left *quan* 颧 (left cheek)
47	right *quan* (right cheek)

Age	Area of face
48	*zhun tou* 準头 (tip of nose)
49	left *lan tai* 兰台 (left wing of nose)
50	right *lan tai* (right wing of nose)
51	*ren zhong* 仁中 (depression above upper lip)
52 & 54	left *xian ku* 仙库 (left area above upper lip)
53 & 55	right *xian ku* (right area above upper lip)
56	left *fa ling* 法令 (line on left inner cheek)
57	right *fa ling* (line on right inner cheek)
58	left *xuan bi* 悬壁 (area of cheek below left ear)
59	right *xuan bi* (area of cheek below right ear)
60	*zheng kou* 正口 (mouth)
61 to 63	*di ku* 地库 (area below lower lip)
64	left *po chi* 波池 (area on left of left *fa ling*)
65	right *po chi* (area on right of right *fa ling*)
66	left *jin lu* 金娄 (tip of left *fa ling*)
67	right *jin lu* (tip of right *fa ling*)
68	left *gui lai* 归来 (area below left *jin lu*)
69	right *gui lai* (area below right *jin lu*)
70 to 73	*di ge* 地阁 (chin)
74 to 75	*sai gu* 颐骨 (areas flanking *di ge*)

2 The Face

According to Chinese belief, the countenance depicts the emotions and passions of man but the shape, form and proportion of the skull show his intellectual power and sensibility. Even though man ages with passing years and his face wrinkles, his skull remains basically unchanged.

The Chinese face reader classifies 10 desirable shapes of the face, namely, *feng*, *mu*, *shen*, *tian*, *tong*, *wang*, *jia*, *yong*, *yuan* and *you*. Irregularly shaped or deformed faces are considered undesirable. Generally these shapes can be broadly divided into three, namely, square, triangular, and oval or round. Square-shaped faces include *feng*, *mu*, *tian*, *tong*, *wang* and *yong*. Triangular faces include *jia* and *you* while oval are *shen* and *yuan*.

Generally it is believed that people with square-shaped faces have positive and forward personality traits. Elongated faces indicate creativity, positiveness and confidence. Peope with narrow faces are creative and artistic whereas round-faced people are financial wizards.

The significance of each of the classified shapes in Chinese face reading is listed on Chart A on page 26.

Hong Kong actor
Kenny Bee has
a mu *face.*

Chart A: Significance of face shapes

Shapes	Significance
feng 风	intelligence, reliability, practicality, assertiveness, stubbornness, endurance
mu 目	strength of character, resourcefulness, assertiveness, creativity
tian 田	endurance, stability, conscientiousness, forthrightness
tong 同	steadfastness, kindness, faithfulness, endurance
wang 王	dedication, persistence, discipline, success, achievement
yong 用	ambition, dependence, apprehension, sensitivity
jia 甲	intelligence, imagination, patience, ambition, intuitivity
you 由	independence, self-assurance, assertiveness, demanding
shen 申	intelligence, luck, determination, flexibility, dynamism, strength
yuan 圆	wealth, happiness, kindness, tact, spirituality

The *feng* face is wide and appears quite squarish and short. It belongs to one who has a high level of intelligence and endurance. The person may also be stubborn and assertive. Few with a *feng* face are known to give up their plans or are found unreliable. Actress Angela Lansbury, of *Murder She Wrote* fame, has a *feng* face.

Angela Landsbury ▶

The *mu* face belongs to one who has strength of character, assertiveness, and he is resourceful and creative. It is slightly rectangular and long. One who has a *mu* face is a good leader and diplomat. He is usually respected for his inventive ideas and creative work. The late Chinese premier Zhou Enlai had a *mu* face, so has Hong Kong actor Kenny Bee.

Late Chinese premier ▶
Zhou Enlai

The *tian* face is squarish with wide jaws and temples. It belongs to one who has a great endurance and fortitude, with a conscientious and forthright nature. Many good soldiers and military leaders had *tian* faces. Few women have *tian* faces. An unusual example is Hong Kong actress Zhang Man Yu.

Zhang Man Yu ▶

Hong Kong actor Chou Yuen Fatt has a tong *face and thoughtful and expressive eyes.*

Singapore actress Ling Li Yun has a jia *face.*

The *tong* face is almost rectangular. It belongs to one who is kind, humane, faithful and loyal. People with *tong* faces are also steadfast in their work, calm and able to endure hardship. Hong Kong actors Zhang Zhao Hui and Chow Yuen Fatt have a *tong* face.

Zhang Zhou Hui ▶

The *wang* face is rectangular with prominent forehead and chin. It belongs to one who is dedicated to his work and persistent in his pursuit of excellence. One who has a *wang* face is usually a born leader, disciplined, resourceful and he usually succeeds in his work. Hong Kong actor Wang Shu Chi has a *wang* face.

Wang Shu Chi ▶

The *yong* face which is long and narrow belongs to one who is resourceful, creative and assertive. The person with a *yong* face is not terribly good at concealing hurt feelings. Few people have a *yong* face because it is slightly irregular. American actor John Carradine had a *yong* face.

John Carradine ▶

The *jia* face belongs to one who is intelligent and intuitive. The *jia* face has a wide forehead and a narrow jaw. One who has a *jia* face is sensitive and imaginative. He is also ambitious and aims high. Hong Kong actress Zhou Hai Mei and Singapore actress Lin Liyun have a *jia* face. (See page 28.)

Zhou Hai Mei ▶

The *you* face has a narrow forehead and a wide jaw. It belongs to one who is independent, confident and assertive. One who has a *you* face is usually happy and relaxed. Hong Kong actress, Lydia Sum, has a *you* face.

Lydia Sum ▶

The *shen* face has prominent cheek bones but a pointed and small chin. It belongs to one who is intelligent, determined, dynamic and reliable. One who has a *shen* face is flexible and adaptable. American actress Brooke Shields has a *shen* face.

Brooke Shields ▶

The *yuan* face is round and sometimes slightly plump. It belongs to one who is kind, tactful and contented. One who has a *yuan* face is usually positive and looks at things on the brighter side. Singer Li Lan Feng has a *yuan* face.

Li Lan Feng ▶

Although 10 shapes of the human face have been listed, there are numerous variations and combinations of the listed shapes. For example, there are shapes that are a combination of *feng* and *mu*, *tian* and *tong*, *wang* and *yong*, *jia* and *mu*, *you* and *feng*, and so on. Combination of face shapes means a combination of characteristics.

The face can be divided into three zones: the upper zone which is the upper part of the face just before the eyebrows, the middle zone which is from the eyebrows to the tip of the nose, the lower zone which is from the tip of the nose to the chin (see diagram below).

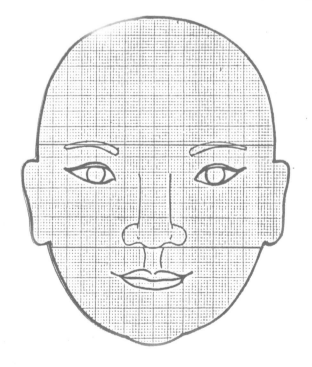

The upper zone indicates luck at youth (including parental support). This area should be wholesome, full and free from marks or spots to indicate intelligence.

The middle zone indicates luck from 31 to 50. This area should be well-formed to indicate health, fortune, productivity, power and success.

The lower zone indicates luck from 51 to 71. It should be well-proportioned to indicate family happiness and good retirement and health.

The three zones of ex-tennis star Bjorn Borg's face are almost equal.

The upper zone denotes the mental and intellectual capacity of the person and the luck of a person from the age of 15 to 30. The middle zone denotes fortune and capability and the luck of a person from age 31 to 50. The lower zone denotes financial security and wellbeing after the age of 50. The three zones should be equal in height (see photograph of ex-tennis star Bjorn Borg whose three facial zones are almost equal).

In addition to the three zones, the face is further divided into eight regions, each region governing an aspect of life. The eight regions and their spheres of influence are as follows (refer also to diagram):

1   forehead — profession and job

2   *yin tang* (area between the eyebrows) — ambition

3   *ling yun* (areas above eyebrows) — family

4   *xiao yin* and *xiao yang* (outer tips of right and left eyes respectively) — marriage

5   *quan* (cheeks) — society

6   nose — health and luck

7   areas above and below mouth (including chin) — food and home

8   *qian yi* (left and right sides of forehead) — travel

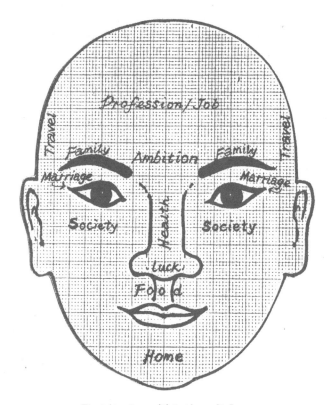

The eight regions and their spheres of influence.

● The forehead governs the career, profession and how the person gets on with his job. Achievement, accomplishments and success are depicted by a smooth and well-formed forehead. An indented forehead or deformed forehead indicates slow progress and advancement in career. (See well-formed foreheads of Mahatma Gandhi, the man who led India's fight for independence, Prime Minister of Britain Margaret Thatcher and English novelist of the 19th century, Charles Dickens, in chapter on foreheads.)

● *Yin tang*, the area between the eyebrows, governs the ambition and drive of a person. This is an important area because with drive and perseverance, one is likely to succeed. It should be smooth, wide and without defects or marks. Narrow or deformed *yin tang* indicates easy sociability, lack of interest and setbacks in life. *Yin tang* with wild hair depicts a selfish and unforgiving nature which leads to negativeness and lack of ambition.

33

● The areas above the eyebrows should be free from marks that mar or disfigure. They govern family life, filial piety and love between family members. They also reveal family influence and inheritance. If there are deformity or marks, the person may not have good family backing.

● The outer tips of the left and right eyes govern marital happiness. Defects occurring on these areas may indicate problems concerning marriage partners.

● The *quan* or cheeks indicate how society treats the person and how he interacts with his friends. If the cheek bones are strong and well-formed he makes good lasting friendship with people and he enjoys rapport and support from his friends and superiors.

● The nose depicts the health and luck of a person. Deformity and wrinkles on the nose depict poor health and ill luck. An extremely thin nose with exposed nostrils indicate ill luck and empty bank accounts.

● The areas above and below the mouth depict the home life which includes food and comfort. If these areas are deformed the person suffers emotionally from having a broken home or may have hardship in life.

● The *qian yi* or sides of the forehead depict how much the person travels and gain experience and wealth from overseas ventures.

The Qin dynasty encyclopedia, *Gu Jin Tu Shu Zhi Cheng*, dated 1726, has the following record on face reading:
大凡观人之相貌，眉目之清秀，看神气之荣枯，取手足之厚薄，观须发之踈浊。

Translated, it means: in face reading, read the clarity and refinement of the eyes and eyebrows; look for the glow or the withering of *shen qi* (spirit and energy) and examine the hands and feet to see if they are thick, look for the scarcity or abundance of hair and beard.

3   The Ears

The ear consists of an inner ear which cannot be seen, and an outer ear which can be seen. The outer ear is analysed in face reading. The ears govern the fortune of ages 1 to 14.

The personal traits as well as destiny for a male from 1 to 7 years old can be assessed by looking at the left ear and from 8 to 14, at the right ear. For a female, the right ear is analysed for ages 1 to 7 and the left, for ages 8 to 14.

The length, shape and profile of the ear are believed to depict the life span, personality traits and ambitions of a person. The longer the ears are the longer the life span and the better fortune enjoyed by the person.

If the upper portion of the ear is large or larger than the lower portion, it indicates intelligence and strong memory. If the middle part is wider than the upper and lower parts then it indicates strong creativity and intellectual capacity. If the lowest part is fleshy and as wide or big as the upper parts it indicates compassion and patience. The shapes of ears identified in face reading are rectangular, pointed, long and round (see chart on page 36).

The length and shape of the ear may suggest the personality traits but the profile and thickness of the helix and lobe depict the luck and opportunity of the person. The more fleshy the ear the more luck and security available. Thin and twisted ears signify poor luck and very badly formed ears depict a disturbed personality.

The shape of the ears is not likely to change over the years although they tend to grow slightly longer.

The position of the ears in relation to the eyebrow height defines the

Shape of ear		Characteristics
Rectangular		honest, compassionate, intelligent, stable
Pointed		shrewd, sensitive, intuitive, alert
Long		determined, honest, conservative, long lived
Round		artistic, creative, good natured, appreciative of cultural activities

◀ *A thin and twisted ear.*

A badly formed ear. ▶

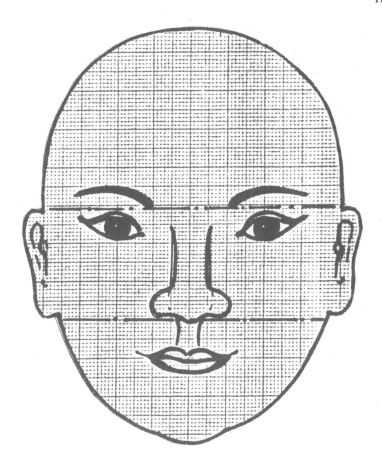

*The ideal position of the ear
is just below the eyebrow and above the tip of the nose.*

character of the person. The ideal position is just below the height of the eyebrow and just above the tip of the nose (see sketch above).

Ears which are below the eyebrow and above the tip of the nose indicate that the person is honest, kind, intelligent and patient. A person with ears above the eyebrow is egoistic, hot-tempered, ambitious, determined and highly successful.

Ears that are flattish and do not protrude when the face is examined from the frontal view indicate that the person is kind, dynamic, forgiving and fair. If they stick out, the person may be endowed with wealth but his happiness may be marred by conflicts he faces in his personal relationship with others.

However, ears should be proportionate to the face. If the ears are too large, the face looks rather awkward. On the other hand, if the ears are too small, the person may not have the support from others.

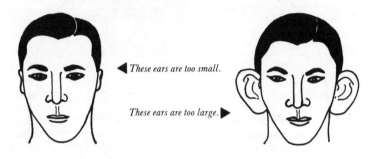

◀ *These ears are too small.*

These ears are too large. ▶

Types of ears and their significance are summarised below.

Types of ears	Significance
ear with good lobe, fleshy, shiny and smooth	brilliance, luck, good family support, determination
ear with a small lobe and is thin, dull and ill-formed	dull, poor luck, poor family background, lacking in confidence
ear with long lobe, well shaped and smooth	long life, wealth
ear without lobe, very short, dry, poorly formed and irregular	short life, poverty
ear above level of eyebrows, with good lobe and well-shaped	wealth, promotion, progress
ear pointed and shaped like a triangle	greedy, immoral, early death for parents

Former President of the United States of America, Ronald Reagan, has long ears that depict longevity and support from his associates and family.

Japanese architect, Minori Yamasaki, has pointed ears.

Francis Chopin, the famous Polish pianist and composer, had round ears and an expressive face that revealed his talents.

David Marshall, well-known crime lawyer, ex-Chief Minister of Singapore, and ambassador to France, has elongated ears and a good lobe.

It is believed that the size of the ears is related to the size of the kidney. The larger the ears the larger the kidneys. The higher the ears, the higher the kidneys are located.

Summing up, it is believed that the shape of the ear should be balanced, close to the head and preferably long and fleshy.

4 The Forehead

The forehead reveals the intelligence and intellect of a person as well as mental attitude. It also shows the fortune of ages 15 to 32.

There are basically two types of profiles for foreheads namely concave and convex. The convex, broad and high forehead belongs to the positive, efficient, intelligent, imaginative and intellectual person. The concave, narrow and low forehead is indicative of a patient, agreeable and easy going person.

Left: A convex, broad and high forehead.

Right: A concave, narrow and low forehead.

There are a few variations of foreheads such as broad, narrow, high, low and average in size. The ideal size is 1/3 that of the face. (See sketch right.)

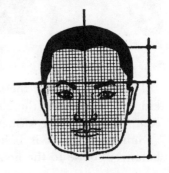

The chart below shows some typical foreheads and their significance.

Type		Significance
high and broad		intellectual, creative, practical, virtuous, forgiving, generous
high and narrow		intellectual, practical, cautious, imaginative
average		intelligent, balanced, inventive, compassionate, sociable, practical
low and broad		practical, athletic, robust
low and narrow		strong minded, not very compassionate, preferring outdoor life

Irrespective of the types of foreheads, the profile of the forehead should be convex, full and free of defective marks.

British Prime Minister Margaret Thatcher has a high and broad forehead, a high nose with small nostrils and firm lips.

Mahatma Gandhi, Indian political leader in the 1940s, had a convex forehead. This profile of him shows that he had a benevolent forehead and resolute nose. He had thoughtful eyes and large protruding ears which were some of the features that depict his long life and his ill fortune of being assassinated at 78.

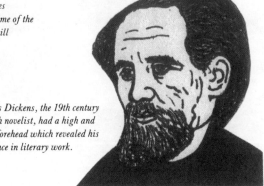

Charles Dickens, the 19th century English novelist, had a high and broad forehead which revealed his brilliance in literary work.

Taiwanese actress Lin Chin Hsia
also has a good and high forehead.

5 The Eyebrows

Eyebrows depict the intellectual and emotional faculties of a person. They also denote the quality of life from age 33 to 34.

Generally, eyebrows should be longer than the eyes and should be well-formed. Fine, arched eyebrows are feminine while rectilinear and bushy brows are masculine.

Long and well-formed eyebrows denote intelligence and gentleness and a strong capacity to cultivate scholastic, cultural and social skills. Eyebrows that are much shorter than the eyes or have scars that mar them depict selfish and crude characteristics.

The hair of the eyebrows indicate the intelligence and compassion of a person. The hair of the eyebrows should be firm and running parallel. Long eyebrows with fine hair signify inner beauty and strength, compassion and sensitivity, intelligence and capability to perform. Short, bushy eyebrows depict practicality and determination but if the eyebrows are not well-delineated with hair growing in different directions, the character may be hot-tempered and impatient. Interrupted eyebrows (those that are marred by a cut or loss of hair) indicate setbacks in life. Wild and overly bushy eyebrows denote a perplexed and wild personality. If the hair of the eyebrow is scarcely grown the person may not be able to keep his savings.

The area of the face between the eyebrows is called *yin tang*. The *yin tang* is preferred to be wide rather than narrow. A wide *yin tang* indicates that the person is broad minded and positive. If it is very narrow so much so that the eyebrows almost meet then the person may be negative and unforgiving. However it should not be too wide or the person may have a volatile personality. The ideal width should be the width of two index fingers laid flat.

Wrinkles on the *yin tang* are indicative of a person's character as indicated in the chart below (see also chapter 10).

Wrinkles	Significance
	decisive, positive, ambitious, practical
	indecisive, negative, temperamental, sensitive

Eyebrows should not be too close to the eyes or the person may be selfish and unforgiving. Below are four types of eyebrows which are not very good.

This eyebrow is not well-formed because the hair is not continuous. It depicts difficulty encountered at the ages of 33 and 34.

This eyebrow is not good because another (smaller eyebrow) grows above it. It depicts danger encountered at the ages of 33 and 34.

This eyebrow is too short and too high above the eye. It depicts a weak character and poor luck.

This eyebrow is too wild and too low over the eye. It depicts a mean character and introvert tendency.

There are many types of eyebrows. The following nine types are the more typical ones.

The *yue mei* 月眉 denotes intellectual brilliance, compassion, emotion and success. It is refined and slightly arched.

The *yi zhi mei* 一字眉 spells success and harmony. It resembles the word *yi* 一 and is rectilinear, straight and refined. It tapers to a point and is longer than the eye.

The *qing xiu mei* 清秀眉 represents the successful and educated. It is slightly arched, tidy, long and refined, tapering to a point and arching over the eyes.

The *hu mei* 虎眉 represents the powerful and outstanding. It is bushy but well-defined, firm and the hair is of constant length.

The *xiao sao mei* 小扫眉 depicts the lonely and independent. It is bushy looking, much like a brush.

The *jian duan mei* 间断眉 represents the average, idle, mean and unforgiving. It is brownish and is broken or marred.

The *ba zi mei* 八字眉 depicts the frustrated although successful. It is slightly slanting and looks like the character *ba* 八.

Singapore singer Anita Sarawak
has brilliant eyes and matching
eyebrows.

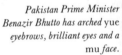

Pakistan Prime Minister
Benazir Bhutto has arched yue
eyebrows, brilliant eyes and a
mu face.

Hermann Goering, Hitler's air minister, committed suicide after being sentenced to death in the Nuremburg war crimes trials at the end of the second world war. His eyebrows were very close to his sharp eyes and his lips were very thin.

The *long mei* 龙眉 is good as it spells a well balanced personality, sociable and friendly. It is straight and well formed.

The *shi zi mei* 狮子眉 spells fortune and happiness. It is bushy but the hair is fine and well formed.

6 The Eyes

The eyes are analysed for the fortune of ages 35 to 40. It is also generally accepted that active and vivid eyes depict an active and acute mind. (See photo of popular Taiwan-born singer, Teresa Teng and sketch of Rajiv Gandhi, prime minister of India.) The fire in the eyes depicts emotion, compassion and even hatred. This is why some say that the eyes are the mirror of the soul. The eyes reveal grief and pleasure, disappointment and triumph, wisdom and ignorance, and all feelings good and bad.

The colours of eyes most common among the Chinese are dark brown and black. The darker the colour, the more brilliant the person. However, the proportion of white compared with the iris (the round coloured part of the eye) is also an important consideration in analysing the eyes. (See sketches below for well-proportioned and ill-proportioned eyes with reference to the 'whites'.)

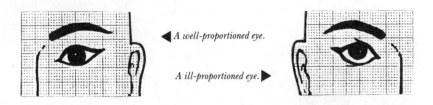

◀ *A well-proportioned eye.*

A ill-proportioned eye. ▶

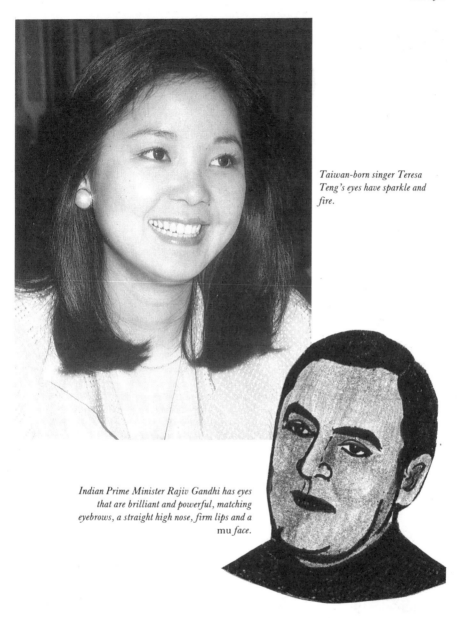

Taiwan-born singer Teresa Teng's eyes have sparkle and fire.

Indian Prime Minister Rajiv Gandhi has eyes that are brilliant and powerful, matching eyebrows, a straight high nose, firm lips and a mu face.

Lively eyes with fire together with good delineation depict strength, vigour, good health and vivacity.

Generally there are about 40 types of eyes. The more common ones are shown below. Each type is named after an animal as the Chinese believe that human eyes bear resemblance to animal eyes.

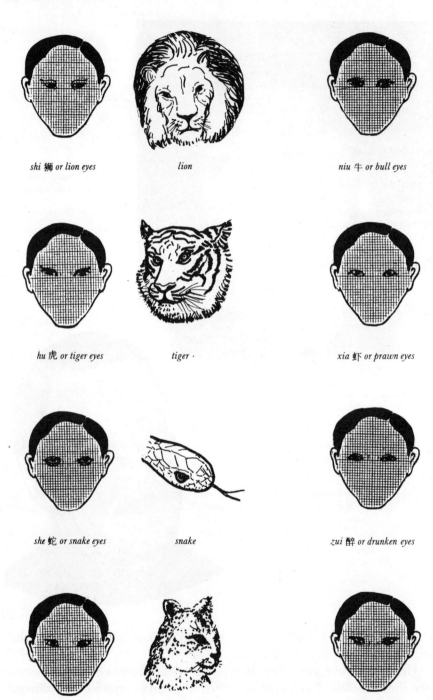

shi 獅 *or lion eyes*

lion

niu 牛 *or bull eyes*

hu 虎 *or tiger eyes*

tiger ·

xia 虾 *or prawn eyes*

she 蛇 *or snake eyes*

snake

zui 醉 *or drunken eyes*

mao 猫 *or cat eyes*

cat

lang 狼 *or wolf eyes*

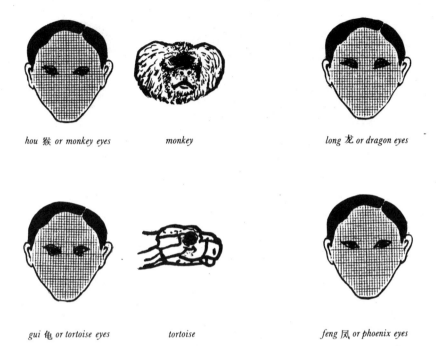

hou 猴 *or monkey eyes*   *monkey*   *long* 龙 *or dragon eyes*

gui 龟 *or tortoise eyes*   *tortoise*   *feng* 凤 *or phoenix eyes*

Generally you can classify the various types of eyes under five categories.

Powerful and intellectual	sleepy and inactive	Sensuous and beautiful	sharp and cunning	honest and sober
long (dragon)	*zui* (drunken)	*feng* (phoenix)	*lang* (wolf)	*niu* (cow)
hu (tiger)	*gui* (tortoise)		*she* (snake)	*mao* (cat)
shi (lion)			*hou* (monkey)	*xia* (prawn)

The relationship of the eyes to the nose and the eyebrows, the slant of the eyes, the size of the eyes, the distance between the eyes, the profile of the eyelids and the spirit of the eyes are just as important as the shape of the eyes. Eyes should be well-positioned. See chart on page 54 on positions of eyes and their significance.

Eyes too large in proportion to face.

Eyes and eyebrows are too slanting.

Imbalanced eyes (one slants more than the other).

Eyes too close to eyebrows.

Eyes slightly slanting.

Eyes too close together and eyebrows too short.

Position	Significance
close together	mean
far apart	generous
close to eyebrows	introverted
slanting	shrewd
big (in relation to face)	naive
small (in relation to face)	secretive
deeply set	cautious
protruding	outspoken
dull	lifeless
shifty	shrewd or dishonest

The white of the eyes should be clear and not bloodshot. Also, if there are 'three whites' the personality traits may be ultrasensitivity, selfishness and high excitability. This woman (right) whose eyes have 'three whites' was found guilty of helping her husband to commit murder and was hanged.

This sketch shows an example of well-delineated, long and spirited eye representing wisdom and intelligence.

This sketch shows eyes that are intelligent and kind.

This sketch shows an example of eyes with protruding eyeballs and small irises which signify danger, ill luck and possibly liver ailment.

This sketch shows eyes positioned too far apart and too slanting representing pessimism and soberness.

7 The Nose

The nose is an important face feature. A person breathes through the nose. When the nose is blocked he suffers and suffocates. This shows how important the nose is in relation to the well-being of the person. The Chinese face reader regards the nose as the 'hill' of the face, generating willpower and representing intellectual capabilities. The nose also depicts the fortune of the ages 41 to 50.

Generally, the nose should be fleshy and not thin, showing the bone structure. The nostrils should be hidden by the *lan tai* or the wings of the nose and the *zhun tou* (nose tip). Pointed and thin noses indicate poor luck and poverty.

There are 20 categories of noses in face reading. Thirteen of them which are the more common ones are featured here.

The *long bi* 龙鼻 or dragon nose belongs to one who is very fortunate and successful. The length of the nose is equal to the forehead. The outline of the nose is well-delineated, neither pointed nor very broad. The nostrils are gently shortened. The *nien shang* (bridge) is straight and firm.

The *shi pi* 獅鼻 or lion nose belongs to one who is highly successful and wealthy. The length of the nose is equal to the forehead. The outline of the nose is well defined but the end of the nose is fleshy and rounded. The nostrils are hardly visible.

The *hu bi* 虎鼻 or tiger nose signifies fame and wealth. The nose is straight in profile but the nostrils are hardly seen and are gently rounded.

The *dan bi* 胆鼻 or gall bladder nose represents wealth and luck. The nose tip is slightly rounded and the nostrils cannot be seen.

The *yang bi* 羊鼻 or goat nose denotes fame and wealth. The nose is straight but the tip of the nose is fleshy and the nostrils cannot be seen.

The *niu bi* 牛鼻 or bull nose denotes peace and comfort. The nose resembles that of a bull although the nostrils are not as large or as exposed as those of the bull.

The *gou bi* 狗鼻 or dog nose represents compassion for others. The nose is not perfectly straight and the nostrils slightly resemble those of the dog.

The *suan bi* 蒜鼻 or garlic nose spells honour and good retirement. The nose resembles a garlic. The tip of the nose is rounded and small.

The *ying bi* 鹰鼻 or eagle nose denotes treachery and cunning. The nose is pointed and its bridge is not straight. The nostrils are set back.

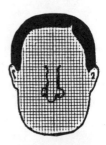

The *hou bi* 猴鼻 or monkey nose spells wealth which does not last. The nose is like that of a monkey with exposed nostrils and skinny, bony bridge.

The *jian bi* 剑鼻 or sword nose represents selfishness and desertion. The bridge resembles a sword as it is very bony. The nostrils are thin and exposed.

The *yu bi* 鱼鼻 or fish nose spells hardship and poverty. The nose is pitched very high and the nostrils are large.

The *lu bi* 鹿鼻 or deer nose denotes wealth and popularity. The nose is slightly pointed and rounded. The nostrils are small.

There are certain basic defects that affect all the categories:

● Moles on the nose are generally not good symbols. They mean setbacks or harsh experiences in life.

● Depressions on the bridge of the nose also denote poor luck or calamities.

● Grey patches on the skin or freckles that suddenly appear on certain areas of the nose also spell ill fortune.

● If the wings of the nose (*lan tai*) are imbalanced, the person may lose his savings at the age of 49 or 50.

Profile of nose

While the shape of the nose viewed from the front generally indicate the fortune of a person, the profile of the nose shows the personality of the person.

This profile belongs to a person who is dynamic, progressive, domineering, practical and stubborn.

This profile shows that the person is artistic, honest, gentle, imaginative and adaptable.

A person with this nose profile is ambitious, skilful in business, shrewd, practical and materialistic.

A person with this profile is soft-hearted, simple minded, contented and unsociable (but if the nostrils are exposed, he or she is extroverted).

Some noses analysed

This nose has a strong bone structure at the upper half and a well-formed lower half consisting of a rounded *zhun tou* which droops slightly downward. The wings on the sides are well-shaped giving ample surround to the nostrils. The muscles of the face at the sides of the nose (including the cheeks) are well-formed. The nose depicts luck, power, intelligence, assertiveness and conscientiousness.

These two noses (see below) are well-delineated with good profiles and well-formed wings covering nostrils. They depict intelligence, luck and a balanced personality.

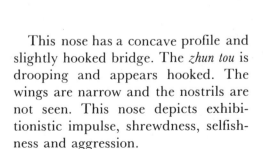

This nose has a·weak root and a convex bridge profile. The *zhun tou* is small and the wings are thin with nostrils exposed. This nose depicts ill luck, insecurity and pessimism.

This nose has a concave profile and slightly hooked bridge. The *zhun tou* is drooping and appears hooked. The wings are narrow and the nostrils are not seen. This nose depicts exhibitionistic impulse, shrewdness, selfishness and aggression.

Summing up, it can be said that the best type of nose is one which is straight and moderately large with a rounded tip. It should be fleshy with nostrils well-concealed. Its bone structure should be straight and its wings balanced and fleshy. Soviet leader, Mikhail Gorbachev, Hong Kong actor, Jackie Chan and the late Duchess of Windsor, Wallis Simpson, all have good and well-shaped noses.

Soviet leader Mikhail Gorbachev has a well-shaped high nose, high forehead, intelligent eyes, firm balanced lips and a mu *face.*

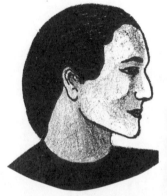

Wallis Simpson (late Duchess of Windsor) had a good nose profile.

Hong Kong actor Jackie Chan has a strong and well-formed nose.

8　The Mouth

Whatever is in the mind of a person is communicated through the mouth. Whatever the heart feels is expressed through it. The Chinese have a proverbial saying *fu cong kou ru, huo cong kou chu* 福从口入，祸从口出 , which in English means good luck (including food) gets in through the mouth and ill luck (including gossips that lead to trouble) gets out through the same mouth. This shows how important the mouth is to a person. To the face reader the mouth (including the areas around it, ie, the *ren zhong*, *fa ling* and *xuan bi* [see chapter 1 for their location]) govern the luck of a person's life from the age of 51 to 60. There are about 20 types of mouths. Eleven common types are described below.

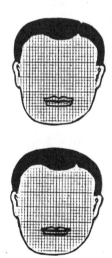

The *si fang kou* 四方口 or square mouth spells fortune and talent. The shape of the mouth is squarish. The upper and lower lips are balanced and the line formed when the mouth is closed is straight. The lips are pinkish red.

The *niu kou* 牛口 or bull mouth denotes wealth and longevity. The shape of the mouth resembles slightly that of the bull. The lips are fleshy and when they are closed a straight line is formed.

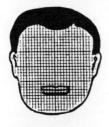

The *long kou* 龙口 or dragon mouth depicts fortune and high office. The lips form a straight line when closed and they are firm and well-defined.

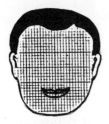

The *hu kou* 虎口 or tiger mouth denotes power and wealth. The mouth is large and curls up very slightly. The lips are balanced, well-defined and slightly fleshy.

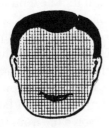

The *yang kou* 羊口 or goat mouth spells poverty. The mouth protrudes slightly and the lips are thin and weak.

The *zhu kou* 猪口 or pig mouth spells ill luck. The mouth is large but the lips are imbalanced. The upper lip protrudes while the lower lip is smaller and set back slightly.

The *yue kou* 月口 or moon mouth represents luck and wealth. The mouth is like a half moon with its ends tilted up slightly denoting an inclination to pleasure.

Gong kou 弓口 or bow mouth denotes wealth and happy old age. It resembles a bow. The lips are fleshy, pink and proportionate, denoting sensuality and compassion.

The *huo kou* 火口 or fire mouth spells poverty. The lips look like those which are blowing on firewood to start a fire. They are protruding and thin. When closed they form a single line denoting coldness and indifference.

The *tao kou* 桃口 or peach mouth represents sensibility and luck. The lips are as pink as peaches and they are small denoting innocence and kindness.

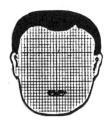

The *yu kou* 鱼口 or fish mouth depicts poverty. The mouth is very small and the lips are hardly seen. The lower lips are slightly hollowed in the middle.

The lips

It is believed that the longer the lips the better the luck and longer the life span. The profile of the upper and lower lips must match. If the upper lip is thin and lower is thick, there is imbalance and the person may also be slightly imbalanced emotionally.

Thin lips depict impulsiveness, hard-heartedness and a cold personality. Lips that are even and balanced in shape and size and whose line tilts upwards depict good luck, self-assuredness, contentment, reliability, intelligence, emotional stability and tenderness.

Profile of lips

When the upper lip is cantilevered beyond the lower, the lips portray insecurity, shyness and unassertiveness.

When the upper lip is set back and the lower lip protrudes, the lips portray selfishness and inconsideration.

When the *ren zhong* (depression above the upper lip) is convex in profile and the lips slightly set back, the lips denote selfishness and materialistic tendency.

When the *ren zhong* is concave in profile and the upper lips protrude, the lips portray indifference and instability in love.

Teeth

Although teeth are not regarded as important in face reading, they should be well-proportioned and of an appropriate size in relation to the mouth. They should be even and balanced in terms of length and spacing.

Protruding teeth are not only ugly but also denote inability to keep wealth. Teeth that are extremely uneven in size and length spell ill luck.

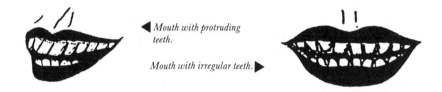

◀ *Mouth with protruding teeth.*

Mouth with irregular teeth. ▶

Ren zhong

The *ren zhong* is the depression just above the upper lip, which ends at the tip of the nose. The length of the *ren zhong* is said to indicate the life span of the person. The longer it is, the longer life one has. If the *ren zhong* is like the character *ba* 八 the person has a difficult period during his early life. If the ren zhong is like an upside down *ba* Ⅵ he has a harder time during his old age. *Ren zhong* should be balanced.

Ren zhong *that resembles the character* ba .

Ren zhong *that resembles an upside down* ba .

Albert Einstein, renowned American physicist who won the Nobel Prize in 1921. He had a fairly long ren zhong *and lived to 76.*

British soccer player Mark Hughes has well-formed fa ling.

Philippine president Corazon Aquino has good fa ling, *balanced lips, well-formed nose, vivid eyes and a* mu *face.*

Fa ling

The *fa ling* or the lines on the inner cheeks which frame the mouth determine one's luck at ages 56 and 57 and show whether one is filial or not. Good *fa ling* should resemble a bell and be balanced. Imbalanced left and right *fa ling* signify early separation from parents and family. If moles are found right on both *fa ling* a person may lose the protection of both parents at an early age. (See photos of Philippine president Corazon Aquino and British soccer player Mark Hughes who have good *fa ling*.)

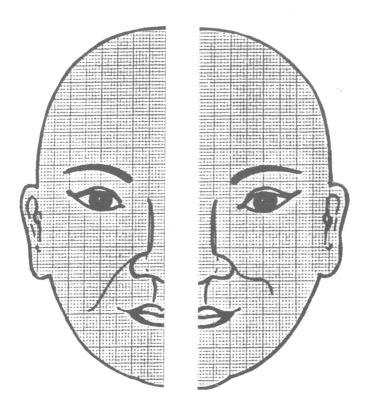

Left: This fa ling *signifies good luck.*   *Right: This* fa ling *signifies happiness.*

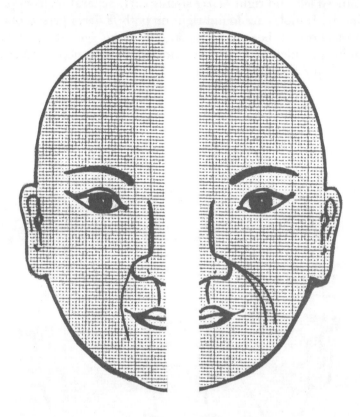

Left: This fa ling *indicates two professions.   Right: This* fa ling *indicates uncertainty.*

9 Cheeks and Chin

The upper parts of the cheeks reveal the fortune of the ages 46 to 47 while the lower parts show the luck of a person of the ages 58 and 59, and from 64 to 67. The chin denotes the fortune of a person from 61 to 75 years of age.

Cheeks

The upper cheeks should be rounded and well-formed with smooth skin. High cheek bones are considered good but they must not be too high either, otherwise the person may be over-dominating, stubborn and proud. High cheek bones also must be accompanied by a strong nose or else success may not come as expected. This is because both the cheeks and nose signify power. Empress Wu Zetian of the Tang dynasty had high cheek bones and so she gained supreme power and was able to maintain it for years.

Cheek bones and their significance are indicated in a chart on page 72.

Cheek bones	Significance
lean and imbalanced	ill health, shy, undisciplined, relaxed
flat	pessimistic, reserved, insecure, complacent, easy sociability
high (with strong nose)	powerful, extroverted, dominating, faithful, careful
low and sunken	weak, introverted, submissive, inconsistent, careless

Chin or *di ge*

The profile of the *di ge* or chin depicts the luck from 61 to 71. Firm, strong and square, and slightly protruding chins are better than weak, pointed and receding chins. Foreshortened chins depict an emotional personality. Strong and expressive chins portray firmness and perseverance. Double chins depict inactivity in sports and games as well as complacency in life. The cleft chin signifies compassion and sentiment. Many sports men have cleft chins, for example, American tennis player, Jimmy Connors.

American tennis player Jimmy Connors.

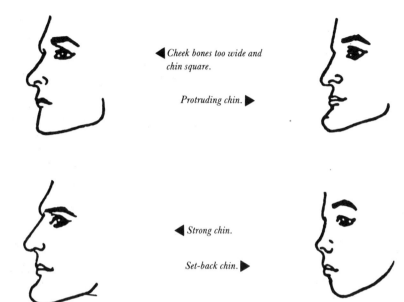

◀ *Cheek bones too wide and chin square.*

Protruding chin. ▶

◀ *Strong chin.*

Set-back chin. ▶

Chin	Significance
square and protruding slightly	brave, enterprising, reliable, forthright (also, healthy stomach)
round and protruding slightly	compassionate, humble, competent, tender (also, healthy stomach)
pointed and protruding slightly	disciplined, imaginative, understanding, trusting (also, healthy stomach)
square and receding	outgoing, openminded, optimistic, complacent (also, strong heart)
round and receding	pretentious, sociable, suspicious, apprehensive (also, strong heart)
pointed and receding	carefree, pessimistic, shy, undisciplined (also, strong heart)

Amadeus Mozart, prolific Austrian music composer of the 18th century, had very prominent jaw and chin. He showed great talent at the age of three, his first work was published when he was seven and he had composed two symphonies by 11. Perhaps his short life (he died at 35) was indicated by the short ren zhong.

Chinese leader Deng Xiaoping has a strong chin which confirms that he remains successful and prominent until a mature age.

American actress Elizabeth Taylor's chin has a good profile. She should enjoy wealth and good life even after retirement.

10   Moles and Wrinkles

Moles

Moles are caused by pigment cells. There are a few types of moles — some are flat, some are fleshy, some have hairs. Some are black, some are brown, and some are very light in colour. Some moles are birth marks while others are developed during childhood or adulthood. To the Chinese face reader, moles are significant indication of luck, good or bad. The following diagrams illustrate favourable and unfavourable moles on males and females. (See pages 76 to 79.)

Wrinkles

Wrinkles that indicate good luck are on the forehead in three parallel lines and they are even better if a vertical one crosses them. They should be firm and continuous. Broken wrinkles or lines are not as good. If there is only one single wrinkle across the forehead, it spells poor luck at the later part of life.

Significant wrinkles on the *yin tang* signify power and longevity.

Wrinkles at the outer tips of the eyes indicate marital happiness. Crosses indicate possible conflict between husband and wife. Wrinkles on the *shan gen* (area of nose between the eyes) depict possible extra marital relationships.

It is a good sign to have wrinkles or lines on the lips as they depict compassion and generosity. Sketches below show favourable and unfavourable wrinkles. (See pages 80 and 81.)

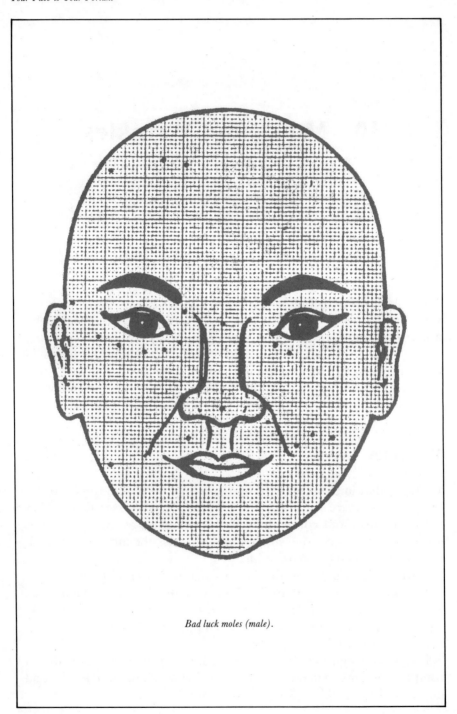

Bad luck moles (male).

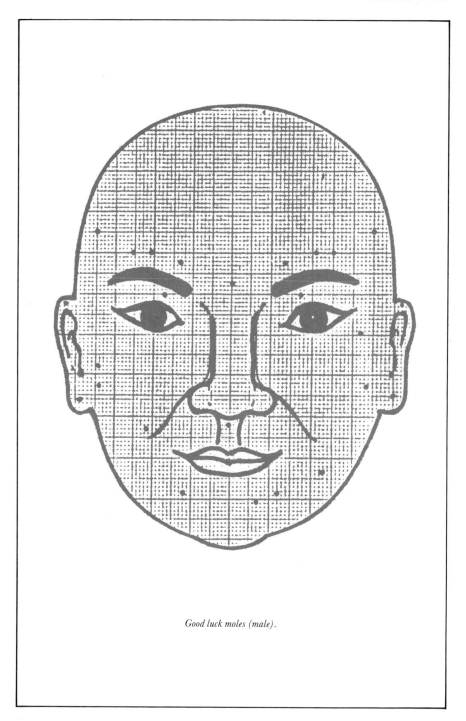

Good luck moles (male).

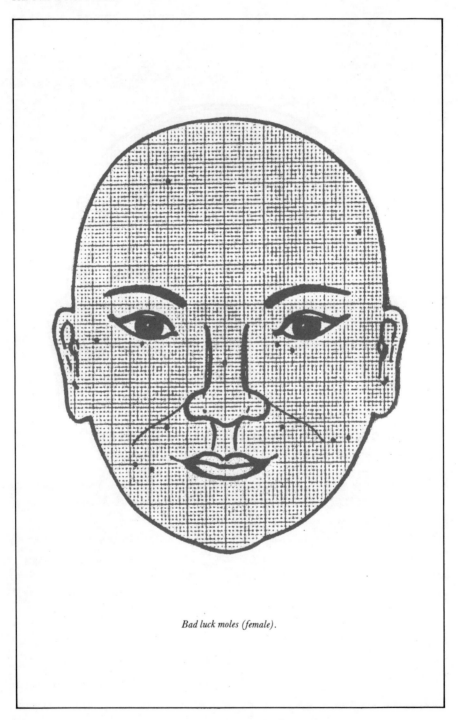

Bad luck moles (female).

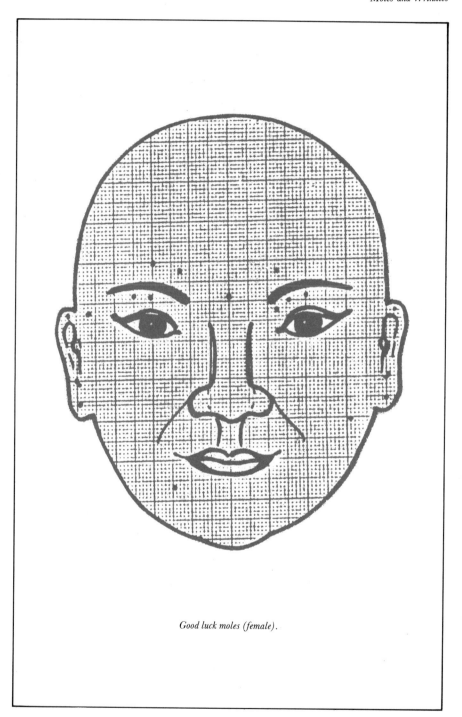

Good luck moles (female).

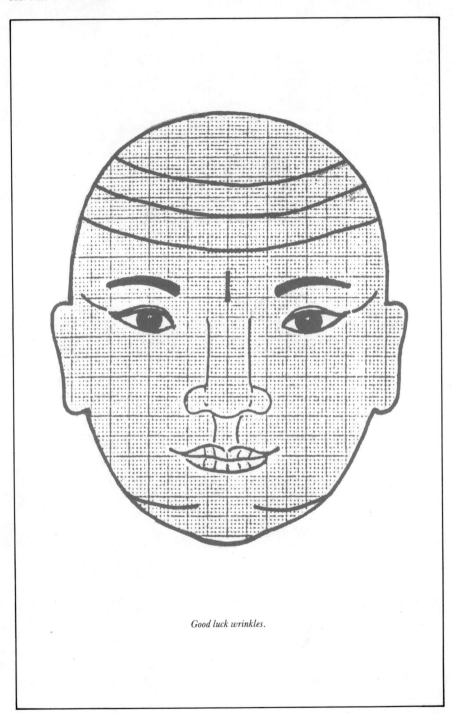

Good luck wrinkles.

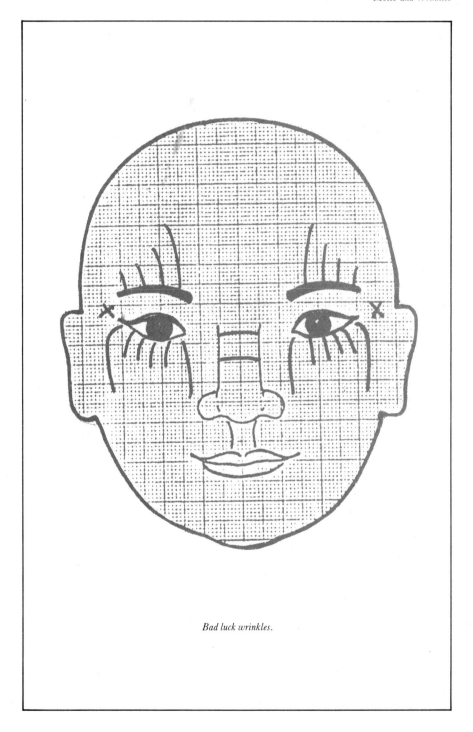

Bad luck wrinkles.

11 Other Aspects of Face Reading

Face reading is not confined to reading the facial features alone. The face must be assessed with *qi* 气 (energy), *shen* 神 (spirit), *gu* 骨 (bone) and *sheng yin* 声音 (voice). Even longevity may not be achieved though the facial features are good but if the *qi*, *shen*, *gu* and *sheng yin* are lacking in quality.

Shen and *qi*

Shen is the spirit hidden behind the physical facial features. It can be detected by looking at the colour of the face and the spirit of the eyes. Spirited eyes (ie, bright, shining eyes) indicate vigorous *shen* while dull eyes reveal dissipated and exhausted *shen*. *Qi* is the energy of the body expressed by the colour and texture of the face.

It is difficult to separate *shen* and *qi*. Together *shen qi* is expressed on the face through its colour and texture. Smooth texture of the face reveals adequate *shen qi* in the person whereas rough and blemished texture indicates poor *shen qi*.

The colour of *shen qi* which is shown on the face tells the wellbeing and fortune of the person. There are five colours on a person's face, namely, green, black, white, red and yellow. Chart A on facing page shows the significance of the colour of *shen qi*.

There are 12 areas of the face, known as *gong*, that indicate particular relationship between the person and the people around him, or a particular aspect of life. (See facing page.)

82

Chart A: Colour of *shen qi* and its significance

Colour	Significance
Greenish and whitish	worries (but also indicates luck if it appears on certain areas. See chart on page 85.)
Blackish	illnesses
Reddish	disagreement (but also indicates luck. See chart on page 85.)
Yellowish	auspiciousness

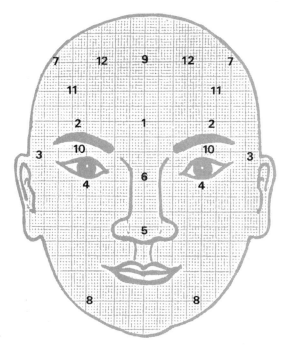

The 12 areas of the face and what they indicate.

The relationship governed by these areas are:

1   fate

2   brotherly love

3   marital bliss

4   relationship with children

5   wealth

6   sickness and calamity

7   housing and settlement

8   employee/employer relationship

9   political powers

10   property

11   virtues

12   relationship with parents

If these areas are favourable as described in the earlier chapters, then the relationships or aspects of life represented would generally be good. However, if spots or discolourations are found on these areas (showing poor *shen qi*) there could be problems encountered.

Generally, the various areas on the face are also representative of the 12 lunar months in a year. Each area is associated with colours. See sketch of face to find out the area of face associated with the lunar month, and then the chart that follows to find out the favourable or unfavourable colours.

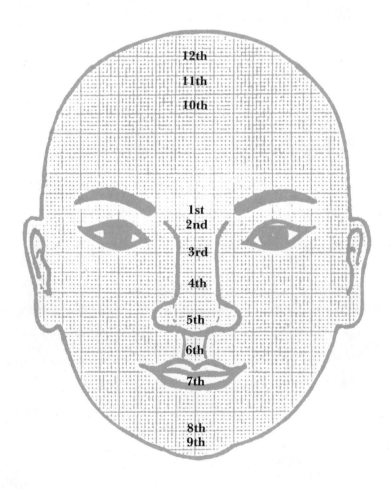

The 12 areas of face that represent the 12 lunar months.

Lunar Month	favourable colour	unfavourable colour
1st	greenish or reddish	white or yellowish
2nd	natural colour of skin	white or greenish
3rd	reddish	white or greenish
4th	reddish	white or greenish
5th	yellowish or reddish	greyish
6th	natural colour of skin	greenish
7th	natural colour of skin	greenish
8th	yellowish	grey
9th	natural colour of skin	reddish
10th	natural colour of skin	reddish
11th	natural colour of skin	dark grey
12th	natural colour of skin	dark grey

Generally, certain colours signify poor health for certain areas, as shown in the chart below and on page 86.

Area	Colours showing poor luck and health
forehead	grey, green, reddish (heart ailment)
yin tang (area between eyebrows)	green (lung ailment), red, white, grey (heart ailment)
shan gen (area of nose between eyes)	grey, green (liver ailment)
nose	green (liver ailment), red (spleen ailment)

Area	Colours showing poor luck and health
area above eyebrows	white (lung ailment)
area surrounding eyes	grey, green (lung or spleen ailment)
cheeks	grey or red (kidney ailment)
ears	grey (kidney ailment)
mouth	green, grey or too red (heart ailment)
di ge (chin)	grey, green (stomach ailment)

Grey and greenish colours depict misfortune especially when they occur on the *shan gen* (area of nose between eyes) or around the eyes. Yellowish colour indicates possible ill health but if it occurs at the *zhun tou* (tip of nose) up to the *yin tang* (on the nose) it depicts progress and luck. Pinkish colour on the cheeks depicts luck and romance. Although reddish colours are generally good, if they occur in a concentrated area or in a deep line on the nose or *shan gen*, they depict danger.

Colour of the eyebrows should be even. This means that the hair of the eyebrows should have the same intensity of colour throughout. Colour of the *yin tang* should not be greyish or marred by discolouring or else the person may encounter calamities or setbacks in life. If red spots occur on the *yin tang* the person may have disputes that end in the court house.

Generally the colour of the face plays an important part in the indication of the person's health and mental state. It should generally be of even colour (although there are preferred colours, see page 87). The face should not have patches of discolouring or marks or spots.

Left: favourable colours.

Right and bottom: unfavourable colours.

Gu (bone)

How does one assess the bone structure in face reading? Ancient writings have the following to say:

- The bone structure should be well covered by the flesh. If the bones show, the person is not outstanding.

- The important bone profiles on the face are the forehead, eyebrow and cheeks.

- The amount of the flesh on the bones must be balanced. For example, if the person is thin the flesh covering the bone structure of the face should not be too thick.

Sheng yin (voice)

How is sound assessed? Ma Yin, a famous face reading master, said the following.

人之有声，如锺鼓文有响，
器大则声宏，器小则声短，
神清则气和，气和则声深而圆畅也
神浊则气促，气促则声急而轻嘶也

Translated, the above means — a person has a voice just like a bell or drum making sound. Big vessel makes loud sound and small vessel, short sound. Pure spirit has harmonious *qi* (energy) which produces deep and smooth sound. Impure spirit has impatient *qi* which produces interrupted sound.

In face reading, the sound that comes out of the mouth should come from the *dan tian* (below the navel) and the speech should be clearly made.

12   Some Famous Faces Read

Introduction

The earlier chapters show how a person's personality traits and his fortune are indicated in particular areas of his face. Facial features such as the forehead, the eyebrows, the eyes, the nose, the ears, the mouth, the cheeks and chin, not only reflect the inner self, but also reveal the fortune, good or ill, of a person. The good face is not just the pretty or handsome face. The facial features must be good in accordance with the theory of face reading.

Numerous real life examples have been given to help one get to know people better by reading their faces. More examples are given in the following pages, in the form of famous people through the ages from 551 B.C. to our century. Their facial features are analysed with reference to the milestones in their lives, to their successes and failures.

Years of age referred to in this section are calculated according to the Western calendar. For example, Confucius, who was born in the year 551 B.C., was one year old in 550 B.C. and not two years old.

Confucius 孔夫子(551 to 479 B.C.)

Nationality: Chinese
Occupation: philosopher, teacher,
             writer

Milestones in life:
Lost his father at the age of three. He
was a self-made man. At 15, he worked
as a clerk in the Memorial temple of
the Duke of Zhou. At 21, he was one of
the Secretaries of Justice at the impe-
rial court. After his resignation he travelled widely. At 67 he retired at
Lu. For five years he edited the famous *Wu Jing*, the *Five Canons of
Confucius* (including the *Book of Changes*, the *Book of History*, the *Book of
Poetry*, the *Book of Rites* and the *Book of Spring and Autumn*). He died at
72.

Analysis of facial features:
From Confucius' face it can be detected the qualities of good human
nature such as humility, love, magnanimity, honesty, determination
and generosity. Although his childhood was not a period of enjoyment
materially, he was much inspired by his mother spiritually. His
forehead and ears revealed such spiritual encouragement, and his
personal achievement at 21. Although his life from 40 to 67 was not a
period of idleness and enjoyment, his travels enriched his knowledge
and wisdom. These were depicted by his nose, mouth and lips. His
achievements from 67 to his death were just as great. He wrote and
edited the *Wu Jing* which earned him recognition as a theorist and
teacher.

Gaius Julius Caesar (100 to 44 B.C.)

Nationality: Roman
Occupation: politician, general,
        statesman

Milestones in life:
Born in 100 B.C. of noble family. His
father died when he was 16. He was
brought up by his dedicated mother.
At 22, he became a prosecuting advo-
cate. At 31, he was promoted but his
wife died. At 37, he was made pontifex maximus (supreme pontiff of
the highest religious authority).

As general, he won many victories, including the conquest of Gaul.
At 51, in a civil war, he drove his political opponents out of Italy. He
later proclaimed himself dictator.

Although he was very strong physically, his life was put to an end
when he was brutally murdered at the age of 56.

Analysis of facial features:
From Caesar's facial features it can be detected that he was brilliant
(his eyes were large and intelligent). He was hard (his lips were not
balanced, with thin upper lip and thick lower lip, and his nose was not
really straight). He was also very determined (see his firm lips and
bushy eyebrows). His forehead and ears confirmed his good upbringing and powerful family background. He had a powerful nose and
won many victories from the age of 40 onwards. His left *fa ling* and
hollow cheeks indicated his violent death at 56.

Cao Cao 曹操 (155 to 220 A.D.)

Nationality: Chinese
Occupation: politician

Milestones in life:
He was born in 155 A.D. into a family of wealth and power. At 20 he took office as attending officer of Emperor Han Xi. Later he was sent to Luoyang as an administrator. At 29, there was internal revolt so he was assigned the duty as military leader. In 189 A.D., the Emperor passed away but his successor was only 14, so Dong Zhuo, the evil Rector of the imperial court, assumed power and appointed another emperor who was only nine years old. Cao Cao retired and left the capital. However, to regain power he sought the alliance of others and formed a military power to challenge Dong Zhuo.

At 41, Cao Cao became a very powerful military leader. At 53, he became Prime Minister. He died at 66.

Analysis of facial features:
Cao Cao had long and well-formed ears which depicted his powerful family background and good upbringing. His forehead was extensive and well-formed — at 20 he was offered a post by the emperor. His *yin tang* (area between eyebrows) was full and his eyebrows are quite far apart. Thus there was a change in his life, a turning point, which led him to hold military power later on. His nose spelt power, luck and determination, thus, from 40 to 50, he became powerful, influential and successful. His weak features were his thin lips. He did not live beyond 66.

Zhu Geliang 诸葛亮 (181 to 234 A.D.)

Nationality: Chinese
Occupation: general, political adviser

Milestones in life:
He lived a life of a recluse until he was 27. Internal war broke out when he was three years old. He ran away, when he was a youth, from his home-town to stay with his uncle. But when he was 17, his uncle died.

When he was 27, a feudal lord, Liu Bei, went personally three times to his hut to urge him to become his political adviser. He agreed and by the age 40 he became Prime Minister to Liu Bei. He led a highly successful and accomplished life. He died at 53.

Analysis of facial features:
Zhu's forehead was ordinary and his eyebrows were rather short, thus his life during his younger days, from 3 to 17 was a hard life, full of turmoil and disappointments. But his eyes were well-formed and he reached the peak of his career by the age of 40, when he became Prime Minister. He was brilliant, intelligent and resourceful, but he lived a short life as his *ren zhong* was rather short.

Empress Wu Zetian 武则天 (624 to 705 A.D.)

Nationality: Chinese
Occupation: empress during the Tang
dynasty

Milestones in life:
Born in 624 into a powerful family.
Her father was a government official
and her mother was the daughter of a
former prime minister of the Sui
dynasty which preceded the Tang
dynasty. When she was 11, her father died and she and her mother
were ill-treated by her father's first wife. At 14, she was brought into
the imperial household as a concubine of Tang Tai Zhong. She was
lonely from 14 to 26 although she was living in the palace. When she
was 25, the emperor died and she was sent to a nunnery. At 28, she
was readmitted to the palace as a concubine of the emperor Tang Gao
Zhong. At 42, she became empress and ruled the country until her
death at 80.

Analysis of facial features:
Empress Wu's forehead and temple were full and broad showing that
she was born to a wealthy and powerful family. Her left ear could
have had a defect as her father died when she was 11. Her luck turned
when she turned 28 (see her *zheng zhong* [lower forehead] and *yin tang*
[area between the eyes] which were well-formed). Her eyebrows were
well-shaped and her nose, straight and prominent. Thus her life from
28 to 50 was successful. Indeed her crowning moment came at 42
when she rose to the throne (notice her powerful cheeks). Note her *ren
zhong* (depression above the lips) which was very long, indicating her
long and powerful life.

Yue Fei 岳飞 (1103 to 1142)

Nationality: Chinese
Occupation: military general

Milestones in life:
By the age of 28, he was a patriotic warrior serving the Song emperor, Song Gao Zhong. He won numerous battles, but in 1141, at the age of 38, he was plotted against by traitors and was disfavoured by the emperor. The following year, he was framed by his enemies and executed.

Analysis of facial features:
His forehead was broad and full and he had the support and love of his mother and family. Before he joined the army, his mother tattooed four characters on his back: *jin zhong bao guo* 尽忠报国 , meaning, complete loyalty to the country. His heroic and courageous nature was shown in his broad forehead and slightly slanting eyebrows (*jian mei*). His eyes were too slanting and not well-delineated. It was not surprising that his luck was bad at the age of 39 when his treacherous opponent killed him.

Politian (1454 to 1494)

Nationality: Italian
Occupation: poet

Milestones in life:
He was born in 1454 to a doctor of law. When he was 10 his father was murdered and his family fortune lost. He studied hard and by 20 he was known for his poems. He created many important classical works but died at an early age of 40.

Analysis of facial features:
Although he lost his father at a tender age, owing to his industry and talent, he was able to achieve recognition at 20. His life improved from then on as was demonstrated by his strong facial features — his eyebrows (*yi zhi mei*) and well-delineated eyes. But his nose was slightly twisted and ill-formed and he lived only to 40.

Ben Jonson (1573 to 1637)

Nationality: English
Occupation: poet, dramatist and
　　　　　　 novelist

Milestones in life:
Born in 1573 a few months after his
father's death. Although he was sent to
a private school, he left at 15 to work
as a bricklayer. He married at about
21. By 25 he was acknowledged for his
works but he (allegedly) killed an actor in a duel and was imprisoned.
At 33, he became more well-known for his works. This was the
turning point of his life. Through intervention of his his friends, he
was released from prison. His success was sustained until he reached
53. At 55, he suffered a stroke. He retired and died at the age of 64.

Analysis of facial features:
Jonson's face revealed his hardship during youth. His eyes and *ba zhi
mei* (eyebrows) depicted frustration and sadness. His nose was
well-formed except that its *shan gen* (part of nose between the eyes)
showed the sign of violence. His forehead with wide temples showed
that he was a great artist and poet. His *zheng zhong* (lower forehead)
was full and so at 25 he began to be known for his works. But his
success was marred when he was accused of felony. His eyebrows
sloped down from the *zheng zhong* and this was not a good sign.
However, his luck changed at 33 and his good and productive period
was shown by his strong and fleshy straight nose. His lips were
well-formed so although he had a couple of strokes he survived them
and lived to 64.

Emanuel Swedenborg (1688 to 1772)

Nationality: Swedish
Occupation: scientist, theologian,
scholar, writer

Milestones in life:
At 22, he graduated from university and travelled through Europe for five years. At 27, he published a scientific periodical. He was famous for his scientific and physiological works and theological studies. He died at the age of 84.

Analysis of facial features:
His long and prominent forehead and extensive temples revealed his early success and brilliance. His inventive qualities were revealed in his eyes and the shape of his elongated head. His prominent and straight nose was well-shaped and high-bridged and the nostrils were hardly seen. This showed that his life from 40 to 50 was full of successes and achievements. His chin was long and his face was elongated so he led a long and fruitful life.

Madame de Stael (1766 to 1817)

Nationality: Swedish
Occupation: novelist, playwright, literary critic, historian, poet

Milestones in life:
She had a happy childhood and was
married at 20 to a Swedish ambassador. She was famous at the age of 22
for her writings on politics and drama.
Her career advanced further at 28, but
she was separated from her husband at 31. By 40 she was politically
important because of her political essays and her leadership of
resistance to Napoleon. She remarried at 44. She became an invalid at
50 and died in 1817, at 51.

Analysis of facial features:
Stael's forehead was full—the upper as well as the lower parts were
well-developed. Thus she was highly intelligent and creative and
became famous at an early age. Her publications included political
essays and literary works. Her eyebrows were very thick and shorter
than her eyes, indicating that she was quite strong headed. Perhaps
that is why her first marriage broke down when she was 31. Stael's
nose was well-formed, proportionate, and centrally placed, and she
gained greater recognition and fame from the age of 40 onwards.
Unfortunately, her *ren zhong* was short and very slightly protruding.
She died at the age of 51.

Charles Summer (1811 to 1874)

Nationality: American
Occupation: politician

Milestones in life:
He graduated from Harvard Law School when he was 23. He left America for Europe when he was 26 and returned to the States when he was 29. He lectured at Harvard for a while and became a senator at the age of 41. He

was successful in his career, but his marriage broke down when he was 55. He died at the age of 63.

Analysis of facial features:
His prominent forehead revealed that his youth was blessed with success and recognition. Thus he graduated from one of the best universities in the United States. His eyes were very close to his nose thus he was away from home at the age of 26 and 27. His lower temples (*shan lin*) were well-defined and formed, signifying his return and obtaining a job at Harvard. His nose was straight, well-formed and prominent and he became famous and remained successful until well over 50.

Sun Yat-sen 孙中山 (1866 to 1925)

Nationality: Chinese
Occupation: first president of the Chinese Republic

Milestones in life:
At the age of 13, he left for America to study. At 17, he went to Hong Kong to study medicine, graduating at 26. He practised medicine in Hong Kong but was very involved in politics. He allied himself with anti-Manchu groups (the Manchu ruled China under the Qing dynasty from 1644 to 1911) to achieve his political goals — to free China from the Manchus. At 45 he returned to China as a national hero and became the first president of the Chinese republic following the overthrow of the Qing dynasty by the Nationalists. Shortly after, he resigned in favour of Yuan Shi Kai. At 47, he attempted to revolt against Yuan but failed and fled to seek foreign aid. He reorganised the Guomingdang (Nationalists) in efforts to bring about national unity. He died at 60 without achieving it.

Analysis of facial features:
The shape of Sun's face (elongated with extensive temples) and the facial features showed his kindness, patriotism and dynamic personality. His forehead, well-shaped, and his ears, large and well-formed, indicated his good upbringing and opportunity to be educated. His *yin tang* (area between the eyebrows) and *ling yun* (areas above the eyebrows) were well-shaped, fully developed, thus he graduated with a medical degree and started to practise medicine at the age of 26. His aspirations, ambitions and drive were expressed in his eyes which were well-delineated. His nose was very well-shaped and delineated (neither pointed nor broad) and he was well-respected, very well-known and he achieved his goals from 40 to 45. He faced setbacks and disappointments at 47 and 48. The lower part of his face was not as good as the upper part. He did not have a very long life.

Joseph Vissarionovich Stalin (1879 to 1953)

Nationality: Russian
Occupation: politician

Milestones in life:
Stalin's father died when he was 11. At 15, he matriculated from school. By 19 he was under the influence of Marxism. At 22 he became a member of the Social Democratic Committee (a communist group). He was imprisoned at 23 for his political activities. Stalin became prominent at 33 and was appointed Commissar of Nationalities. At 43, he became secretary general of the Communist party. At 50 he became premier of the Soviet Union. He died at the age of 74.

Analysis of facial features:
From his forehead it is evident that he did not have an easy life at youth. His *tian ting* (mid forehead) was good so at the age of 19 his life changed for the better. But at the age of 23 he faced a setback for a year, as indicated by the left and right upper foreheads or *bian cheng* which were covered with hair. Luck at 34 was clearly shown on his strong bushy and powerful eyebrows. His prominent nose and eyes spelt leadership from 40 to 50 and showed his tenacity, intelligence and firmness. Even his square jaws and powerful chin revealed his drive and his ambition. He lived to a ripe old age of 74 as evidenced by his well-formed left cheek bone.

Virginia Woolf (1882 to 1941)

Nationality: English
Occupation: writer

Milestones in life:
Her father died when she was 22. She married at 30. She achieved success and fame as a writer, but drowned herself when she was 59.

Analysis of facial features:
Woolf's face was one that showed kindness, tenderness and sensuality. She was creative and methodical. She had a strong and straight nose with the nostrils slightly rounded and hardly seen, thus success was achieved from 40 to 50. Her lips were rather imbalanced, the upper thinner than the lower, and her cheeks were depressed. Thus she could not live beyond 59.

Mao Zedong毛泽东(1893 to 1976)

Nationality: Chinese
Occupation: politician

Milestones in life:
Mao was born in 1893 into a prosper-
ous family in a village in Hunan. At
25, he finished school and left home for
Beijing. He returned in 1919 and
founded the Chinese Communist Par-
ty in 1921. He consolidated his authority during the long march from
1934 to 1935. He became chairman of the party at the age of 38. He
became very powerful and triumphed over the Nationalists in 1949,
establishing the People's Republic of China, at the age of 56. By the
age of 60 his influence grew throughout the Communist orbit. At 73
he retired as Party Chairman of the Chinese Communist Party but
continued to be very influential and initiated the Cultural Revolution
to recreate the revolutionary spirit. It only ended after his death in
1976, at the age of 83.

Analysis of facial features:
The most striking features of Mao's face were his cheek bones, his
forehead, his nose and his big mole on the *di ge* (chin). Mao's face was
essentially the *mu* shape although it was not very long. His face
revealed that he was resourceful, determined and a born leader. He
was able to take setbacks and bounce back with vigour. His forehead
was wide, well-formed and smooth, reflecting that he was born into a
fairly well-to-do family and he was highly intelligent. His eyes showed
vigilance and persuasive powers. They also revealed wisdom and
intelligence. His powerful and straight nose indicated success and
capability from the age of 41 to 50. His prominent *quan* confirmed his
ability to command obedience and respect from his subordinates. The
line of his lips were firm and curved slightly upwards indicating that
his influence would spread beyond his homeland. His *fa ling* and
strong chin confirmed that he had a good life after 50. His famous
mole (below the lips) was a lucky mole.

Bibliography

Chinese

Chen Long 程龙 , *Mian Xiang Shu Chu Bu* 面相术初步 , Taipei, Taiwan (n.d).

Da Mo 达摩 *Shen Xiang Quan Pian* 神相全编 , China (n.d.).

Gu Jin Tu Shu Ji Cheng 古今图书集成 , China, 1726.

Gui Gu Zi 鬼谷子

Guan Shan Yue 关山月 , *Gu Jin Xing Xiang Xue* 古今形相学 , Taiwan, 1981.

Li Shang Shan Ren 李上山人 , *Xing Ge Ren Xiang Xue* 性格人相学 Taipei, Taiwan, (n.d.).

Liang Xiang Run 梁湘润 , *Ma Yi Shen Xiang* 麻衣神相 , Taipei, Taiwan (n.d.).

Ma Yi 麻衣 , *Ma Yi Za Lun* 麻衣杂论 , China (n.d.).

Tai Yi Zhen Ren Shu 太乙真人书, China, (n.d.).

Xian Ji Zi 先机子 , *Liu Nien Qi Se Xiang Fa* 流年气色相法 , Taiwan, 1986.

Xiao Ji 萧吉 , *Wu Xing Da Yi* 五行大义 , China, 600 A.D.

Xu Ling 徐玲 , *Gu Ben Shen Xiang Quan Pian* 古本神相全编 , Taiwan, 1988.

Zhang Yao Wen 张耀文 , *Xiang Shu Xue* 相术学 , Taipei, Taiwan (n.d.).

Xu Gu Shan Ren 需谷山人 , *Tian Xia Di Yi Xiang Shu* 天下第一相书 , Hong Kong (n.d.).

English

Eacker, Jay, *Problems of Metaphysics and Psychology*, Nelson Hall, Chicago, 1983.

Lip, Evelyn, *Chinese Geomancy*, Times Books International, Singapore, 1979.

Lip, Evelyn, *Chinese Beliefs and Superstitions*, Graham Brash, Singapore, 1985.

Lip, Evelyn, *Notes on Things Chinese*, Graham Brash, 1988.

Needham, Joseph, *Science and Civilization on China*, London, 1982.

Schiffman, Harvey Richard, *Sensation and Perception*, John Wiley and Sons, 1976.

Index